First Time

Going to School

Melinda Radabaugh

Heinemann Library
Chicago, Illinois

©2003 Heinemann Library
a division of Reed Elsevier Inc.
Chicago, Illinois

Customer Service 888-454-2279
Visit our website at www.heinemannlibrary.com

Designed by Sue Emerson, Heinemann Library
Printed and bound in the United States by Lake Book Manufacturing, Inc.

07 06 05 04 03
10 9 8 7 6 5 4 3 2

Library of Congress Cataloging-in-Publication Data
Radabaugh, Melinda Beth.
  Going to school / Melinda Beth Radabaugh.
      p. cm. -- (First time)
  Includes index.
  ISBN 1-4034-0227-2 (HC), 1-4034-0466-6 (Pbk.), 1-4034-3814-5 (BB)
  1. Schools--Juvenile literature. 2. School day--Juvenile literature. [1. Schools. 2. First day of school.]
  I. Title. II. Series.
  LB1513 .R33 2002
  372.12'44--dc21

                            2001008298

Acknowledgments
The author and publishers are grateful to the following for permission to reproduce copyright material:
pp. 4, 6, 7, 9, 11, 13B, 14, 15, 17 Brian Warling/Heinemann Library; p. 5 Jay Thomas/Image State; p. 8 Carolee Biddle/Heinemann Library; pp. 10, 18, 19 Greg Williams/Heinemann Library; p. 12 Nancy Sheehan/Index Stock Imagery, Inc.; p. 13T Robert Llewellyn/Image State; p. 16L Robert Lifson/Heinemann Library; p. 16R David Schmidt/Masterfile; p. 20 Richard Hutchings/Corbis; p. 21 Tony Greeman/Photo Edit; p. 22 (row 1) PhotoDisc; p. 22 (row 2) PhotoDisc; p. 22 (row 3, L-R) RDF/Visuals Unlimited, Greg Williams/Heinemann Library; p. 23 (row 1, L-R) Greg Williams/Heinemann Library, Brian Warling/Heinemann Library, Brian Warling/Heinemann Library; p. 23 (row 2, L-R) EyeWire Collection/ Getty Images, Spencer Grand/PhotoEdit, Inc., Thomas A. Heinz/Corbis, p. 23 (row 3, L-R) Greg Williams/Heinemann Library, Catherine Karnow/Corbis, Greg Williams/Heinemann Library; p. 23 (row 4, L-R) Brian Warling/Heinemann Library, Robert Lifson/Heinemann Library, Carolee Biddle/Heinemann Library; p. 24 (L-R) PhotoDisc, PhotoDisc, Greg Williams/Heinemann Library; back cover (L-R) Robert Lifson/Heinemann Library, Brian Warling/Heinemann Library

Cover photograph by Brian Warling/Heinemann Library
Photo research by Amor Montes de Oca

Every effort has been made to contact copyright holders of any material reproduced in this book. Any omissions will be rectified in subsequent printings if notice is given to the publisher.

Special thanks to our advisory panel for their help in the preparation of this book:

Eileen Day, Preschool Teacher
Chicago, IL

Ellen Dolmetsch,
Library Media Specialist
Wilmington, DE

Kathleen Gilbert,
Second Grade Teacher
Round Rock, TX

Sandra Gilbert,
Library Media Specialist
Houston, TX

Angela Leeper,
Educational Consultant
North Carolina Department
of Public Instruction
Raleigh, NC

Pam McDonald,
Reading Support Specialist
Winter Springs, FL

Melinda Murphy,
Library Media Specialist
Houston, TX

We would also like to thank the teachers, staff, and students at Stockton Elementary School in Chicago, Illinois, for their help with this book.

Some words are shown in bold, **like this.**
You can find them in the picture glossary on page 23.

Contents

Why Do You Go to School?

You go to school to learn.

You can learn to read and count.

You can learn to share with friends.

You can have fun at school.

What Kinds of Schools Are There?

Some schools are in a school building.

Some are at **churches, temples,** or **mosques.**

Some schools have children
of all ages.

Other schools have only
young children.

When Do You Go to School?

SEPTEMBER						
Sunday	Monday	Tuesday	Wednesday	Thursday	Friday	Saturday
1	2	3	4	5	6	7
8	9	10	11	12	13	14
15	16	17	18	19	20	21
22	23	24	25	26	27	28
29	30	31				

Most children go to school on **weekdays**.

There is no school on Saturday or Sunday.

Some children stay at school all day.

Other children go only part of
a day.

Where Is Your School?

Schools can be near your home.

Some children walk to school.

Schools can be far away.

Some children ride to school on
a **school bus.**

What Do You Do at School?

At school, you listen to the teacher.

You do school work.

You can paint.

You can play with blocks, too.

What Do You Eat at School?

You can eat breakfast at some schools.

Sometimes there is a morning snack.

You can eat lunch at school.

You can bring your lunch or
buy it.

Who Works at a School?

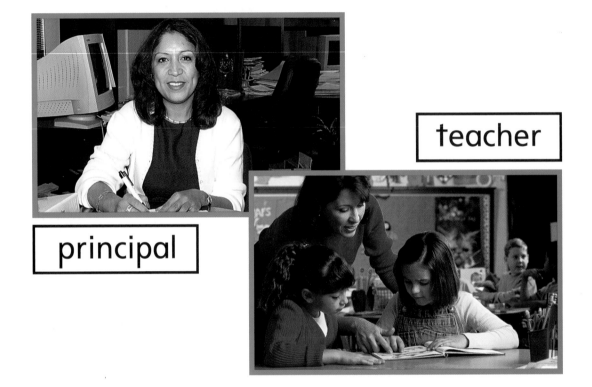

principal

teacher

The **principal** works in the school office.

Teachers work in classrooms.

librarian

custodians

A **librarian** works in the **library**.

Custodians take care of the building.

What Do You Need for School?

A **backpack** holds your papers and books.

Sometimes you bring a toy to show your class.

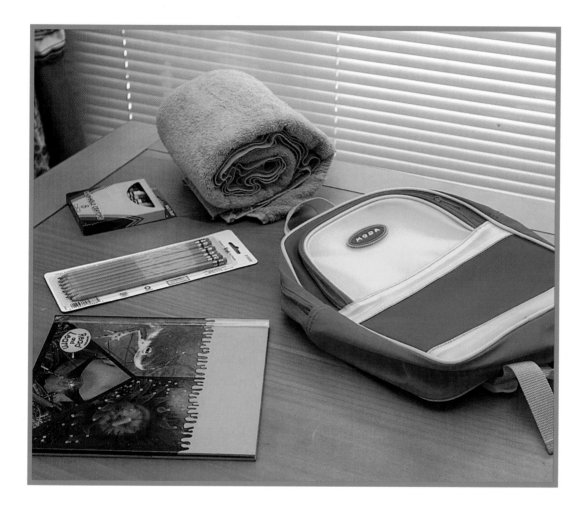

You might need **crayons** and pencils.

You might take a **towel** for a nap.

What Happens at the End of the Day?

You clean up.

You put your things in your **backpack**.

Then, you go home.

Will you go to your house
or a friend's?

Quiz

What goes in your **backpack?**

Look for the answers on page 24.

Picture Glossary

backpack
pages 18,
20, 22

librarian
page 17

school bus
page 11

church
page 6

library
page 17

temple
page 6

crayons
page 19

mosque
page 6

towel
page 19

custodians
page 17

principal
page 16

| Monday |
| Tuesday |
| Wednesday |
| Thursday |
| Friday |

weekday
page 8

Note to Parents and Teachers

Reading for information is an important part of a child's literacy development. Learning begins with a question about something. Help children think of themselves as investigators and researchers by encouraging their questions about the world around them. Each chapter in this book begins with a question. Read the question together. Look at the pictures. Talk about what you think the answer might be. Then read the text to find out if your predictions were correct. Think of other questions you could ask about the topic, and discuss where you might find the answers. Assist children in using the picture glossary and the index to practice new vocabulary and research skills.

Index

Answers to quiz on page 22

| crayons | scissors | pencils |